Keep Moving Forward

Discover the 7 Keys to Transform Your Life

Israel Hernandez

Greatness University Publishers
info@greatness-university.com
www.greatness-university.com

ISBN: 978-1-913164-80-5
ISBN-13: 978-1-913164-80-5

DEDICATION

My first book is dedicated, with love, to my mother Raquel Hernandez. Thank you for always being there for me and giving me advice. You are my superhero.

I also want to thank the members of the San Antonio Elite Toastmasters Club 9434 in San Antonio, Texas, for their guidance and friendship. You are my teachers.

CONTENTS

ACKNOWLEDGMENTS

Writing is a solitary endeavor but producing a book from an idea requires the effort of a team. This book wouldn't exist without hard work, long hours, and a number of people. This book took a lot of baby steps until it became a reality.

To Melissa Dwyer, thank you for helping write this book we started together. To Florence Weinberg, thank you for helping me out. To Scott Avery, thank you for giving me the idea to write a book and believing in me. To my best friend Robert Reyna, if I make it, you make it. To my editor, Matthew Enright, there is not enough words in this world to tell you thank you. Thank you for helping me out with this book, taking time out of your schedule to sit with me for hours, going over the book making a lot of changes, coaching me in so many ways. I have learned so much and grown because of you. To my friends and family, thank you for believing in me.

Foreword

Life is a mystery. Life is full of surprises, some of which make us happy and others turn our happiness into sorrow. The closer we get to understanding life the further it escapes from us. The more we live life the more secrets it reveals. At times we get stuck. We stop and stand still. We cannot see the next step to take on our journey. We are like a person standing on the corner waiting for someone to lead us across the streets of life.

In this life-changing book, Israel tells you that you have the power to change your lifestyle. There is no need to wait. He will give you seven keys to help you transform your life and create your best life.

Some people find it helpful to use analogies to unlock the mystery of life to others. The American writer Carl Sandburg writes, "Life is like an onion. You peel it off one layer at a time, and sometimes you weep." In the film, *Forrest Gump*, Tom Hanks says, "My momma always said life was like a box of chocolates. You never know what you're gonna get." Regardless of what might happen to you, Israel gives you the infallible advice he got from his mother. He advises you and me to Keep Moving Forward.

In this page-turner, he warns us that when things go wrong, we should not go wrong with them. He believes we must refuse to let our past struggles, failures and abuse become our standard. Like the world's number one motivational speaker, Les Brown, Israel believes that there is greatness within each one of us. When we face challenges in life, we have to tap into the greatness within us, anchor onto our true identity and turn our adversities into advantage. Live from the inside out. In my opinion, this requires us to bypass our eyesight and mind-sight and live from a place of **FAITH**. Faith is **F**inding **A**nswers **I**n **T**he **H**eart. In this book, Israel will help you make this transition from eyesight and mind-sight, leading you to the heart where your true identity lives.

If you believe as I do that the solutions to life's problems are found in your heart, then read this. Discover the guidance Israel provides you from the moment you let go of your past to the break-through allowing you to live the rest of your life in its true fullness. If you believe as I do that words have the power to build or destroy, read this book and utter those words that give life, not death, to yourself and those around you. If you believe as I do that to create your best life you need to develop good habits, please read this book and discover how to align circumstances and people to your side so that you become unstoppable as you live your dreams and not your fears.

I now have some questions for you: What do you do when your dreams scare you? What do you do when you are not sure about your identity? What do you do when people do not value you? What do you do when others speak death, not life, to you? What do you do when you are not sure of the habits you need? What do you do when you want to live your best life? What do you do to keep moving forward? My answer is, look at Israel Hernandez. He is a living answer and witness. His book is a page-turner that gives you access to his path as he navigates the challenges of life and makes a safe landing on the positive side. Israel has written this book from his heart to your heart. You have the power to change and discover how never to allow the challenges of life to drag you down. If you believe as I do that it is not over until you win, please read this book and let it transform your life. You have greatness within you. You have the power to keep moving forward and become unstoppable. You have the power to live the rest of your life in its fullness.

~Dr Patrick Businge, Founder of Greatness University and Rewrite Your Future Expert

First Key: Let Go

There Is Power in Letting It Go

As I was growing up, I was always told that I would end up an alcoholic like my dad. I was told that I was never going to accomplish much because I was not born with a silver spoon in my mouth. I grew up as a migrant worker picking corn and strawberries. My parents traveled all over the United States to find work. I had in my mind that I needed to keep my head down and work. This was all I knew as I grew up. My dad would say to me, "If you don't work you don't eat."

In addition, I had a harsh childhood. My father was an alcoholic and used to abuse my mother. From my perspective, he never knew how to love his wife and children. There were no hugs. There were no "I love yous" in our home. Not even once growing up did my dad ever say to his kids "I love you." As a result, I hated my father, and I hated my life. There was no direction and guidance in our home. There was only bitterness, anger, and finger-pointing.

However, one important thing happened that has made me who I am: I knew that in my heart I had to change. I knew there was more to life than hatred, bitterness, and anger. I had to let go of my past, embrace my present, and construct my future. This chapter will give you recommendations on how to let go of your past so that you have a great life for yourself and for those you love most.

Personal Development: Think Differently

In order to grow, I had to let go of my old way of thinking. Let me tell you, it was hard. Very hard. After spending over thirty years of thinking the same way, it felt nearly impossible for me to change. Once I was labelled as a failure, I accepted it. I acted like a failure, and I didn't care about school or my grades. All I wanted to do was party and smoke marijuana. When I was in high school, I got into major fights. I was even expelled from school. Despite this, I eventually got my GED.

I started to change when I began reading books on personal development. A friend of mine gave me my first book. The title was *Rich Dad Poor Dad* by Robert Kiyosaki. This book changed my life. In one of his chapters, Kiyosaki wrote that poor people say poor words, but rich people say rich words. This hit me like a dump truck load of gravel. All my life I was saying to myself "it is okay to be broke as long as I am happy." How many people are living that way? I would see a nice car and say, "Look! He thinks he's all that." Yes, I was one of those kids who would scratch nice cars because I was jealous inside. Deep down I wanted more from life, only I didn't know how to get it. So, I went on a journey to find answers.

Letting Grudges Go

You see, it does not matter what kind of background you come from. We all have something that we have not let go of. There is more to us than we can ever know. Some people will never reach their full potential or rise to their next level in life because they are still holding grudges.

My journey began when I underwent a conversion. I became a believing Christian and came to San Antonio to plant a church. Only two people opened their doors to me. I stayed with them for two days and then I was on my own. It was hard having no family and friends. Even someone I considered a friend did not open his door for me to stay with him. I am very grateful for the people who hosted me for the two nights. Once I was on my own, I had no other choice but to find out how to survive. From that experience, I learned that I must be strong inside.

Have you ever had a situation where you had to survive no matter what it took? I carried grudges for years against the people who did not help me. Somehow, I knew that I could not move on until I forgave those who didn't open their doors for me. So, one day I went for a walk, and I called out every name I knew and said, "I forgive you!" As I was calling out their names, I began feeling better, lighter, and free.

One person I could not forgive was my father. This was still the case even when he passed away. It was not like my parent passing away but more like a friend passing away who had betrayed me. I hated him so much because he was never a father to me. I still remember the time he broke a stick on my back because I was late for dinner. Who would do that to his son? For many years, I carried this anger and hatred with me.

Do you have a friend, brother, sister, parents, whom you've not been able to forgive for years? If you do, then it is time to reconsider and let it go. I did not give myself the chance to do this while my father was alive. One day I went to my father's grave and let it all go. I cursed him. I told him why he was not a great dad to me. I even urinated on his grave. I let out all my anger. Then I cried and told him that I loved him so much. I forgave him. A feeling of peace flooded in my heart. That was a turning point in my life. My father no longer had power over me. My question to you is: who has power over you?

Bob Proctor says that many of us are walking time bombs, ready to explode. Also, many of us are loaded down with dead weight that we've been carrying for years. It's time to let it go. If you want to be free, you need to let go. In this process, you might consider the following questions:

What are the things you need to let go of that have caused you pain?

1._____

2._____

3._____

Who are the people you need to forgive?

Name_____

Name_____

Name_____

From your answers, you can deal with the things you need to let go of and move on. I once interviewed business owners about things they needed to let go of when they started their businesses. Some were surprised at the question I asked. Before you started your business, what past issues did you need to let go of? Here was the response of the first businessman. The fear of failure. His parents always expected him never to make mistakes. He had to be the best in his class, best at football, and when he failed at something his parents would get very upset. Now that he was older, he accepted that everyone makes mistakes.

Another businessman's response was rejection by family and friends. Growing up, he was always bullied by his friends. His parents rejected him because they thought he was the dumbest one in the family. He had low self-esteem and felt unworthy due to his parents' low expectations and lack of encouragement. But he learned that he needed to love himself first and that he needed to see himself as a worthwhile person and later, a father. Letting go takes time. It is not an overnight process.

It is important to note that the number one thing that people don't let go of is unforgiveness. Holding on to anger and bitterness somehow feels like justice, as if you owed me for hurting me. Many people fall into that trap. You feel that you need to pay that person back somehow. That is how people control you. They, too, hold on to unforgiveness because they want you to feel sorry for them. "Poor me, I am hurt!"

I was in that situation with someone for years, until one day I said, no more. I went to that person told her I was sorry, and I walked away. All I could hear was, "you hurt me." I turned and said, "It's your choice now to let it go." I discovered that unforgiveness can destroy a person's health and life by filling them with the poison of bitterness and resentment. I concluded that not forgiving is the worst thing you can do.

I don't know what has happened to you in the past. You might be saying to yourself, "you don't need to know what I have been through or the things I have seen." However, there are lessons everyone needs to learn about forgiveness. Here is what I know about it: failure to forgive can kill you from the inside out like cancer eating you up, sometimes you have to cut ties to the people who hurt you. This can be a hard thing to do when everything inside says otherwise. When it becomes a burden or pain to you, you must choose. For example, I had to let go of people who were not helping me grow even if they were family members.

The next challenging thing to do is to ask for

forgiveness. Imagine so many years of carrying the burden of blaming others for everything, like a heavy backpack. Always blaming. Blaming my parents for not showing love and acceptance. In the end, I had to make a choice and let it go. I had to forgive my parents, including my mother. I vividly remember that day. I was living in Houston, Texas. I was about 22 years old. I called my mother crying and said to her, "Mom, please forgive me for everything I have done to you."

At that moment, I felt I had let go of the burden I had carried in me all my life. There was something so powerful when I let go and she forgave me. It felt like I could breathe again. I also went to other people I had wronged, and I asked them to forgive me. And guess what? They did! Some did not forgive me, but I knew I had done my part. Confronting them face to face was a humbling experience for me, but it was worth it. Unforgiveness would no longer have power over me. I would no longer be a prisoner to my past. No matter if I hurt them or they hurt me, I would still ask for an offering of forgiveness, because I didn't want to carry any more poison in my life.

In his *Book of Manly Men*, Stephen Mansfield writes, "The truth is that forgiving is more about doing than feeling. Forgiving is primarily a decision to treat a wrong and make it a right." It is like the way we cancel a debt of someone who owes us money. We no longer hold the debtor in a debtor's prison. We forgive him or her by deciding that we are no longer owed anything. The record is wiped clean and we have a fresh start. In essence, forgiveness is about doing. You might want to take time and reflect on the people who have hurt you. Make a list of them. Allow yourself to forgive them and set yourself free.

Letting failure go

One of the things I needed to let go of was the fear of failure. This was the hardest for me because all my life, I had always failed. Relatives and teachers used to tell me that I was never going to succeed in life. I remember my fifth-grade teacher telling me, "You will always fail because you come from a broken family. You can't even spell your name right." One day my friends and I skipped class in the fifth grade. I stole twenty dollars from my dad, and we played video games all day long. Yes, I got caught. When I got home, my dad beat the life out of me, but I felt it was worth it. In junior and high school, I got worse. I was labeled as a gang member. I told a teacher once that her job was to help me, but she instead was destroying me. The teacher kicked me out of class. From these experiences, I believed I never would accomplish anything. Wherever I went, failure followed me.

Because of the strong image of failure engraved in my mind for so many years, I never cared about winning. Letting go of this mindset was the hardest thing for me. I knew I had to change that. This journey continued when I listened to personal development and motivational speakers. For example, Les Brown, Zig Ziglar, and Brian Tracy. This set me on the quest to renew myself and to reprogram my mindset.

Have you ever thought of forgiving yourself? Forgiving yourself is as important as forgiving others. Maybe you find it really hard to be honest with yourself about your own faults. You can't admit them, and this holds you back. Be honest! That is often the problem. I believe being honest is an extremely difficult thing to do as well. I really had to come clean. I had to remove the monkey on my back that was weighing me down. One of the things I did was cry. This was my way of letting it all out.

Another way was talking to someone who listened to me. I poured my heart out and laid everything on the table. I hid nothing since I knew I had to confess it all if I wanted to come out clean. It was a hard road, but I was set free. I advise you also to travel that road to forgive yourself, as this is an essential part of healing.

Have you forgiven yourself? Write down the things you need to forgive yourself for. Give yourself time. And be honest here.

Second Key: Find Your True Identity

"The way I am today has nothing to do with what I will be tomorrow." ~Rabbi Daniel Lapin

In the previous chapter, we learned that we cannot hold on to our past, our failures, mistakes, fears, and our pain. It is a hard process, but it must be done to move on to the next level in your life. In this chapter, you will go deep inside yourself to uncover who you really are and who you want to be. Let's get started to find your true identity.

Two questions have haunted me for over 40 years: 'Who are you?' and 'Why are you here?' Finding your identity is vital. There are no two identical fingerprints in this world. Each one is different from the others. Finding your true identity has the power to transform your world and the world around you. When you start finding your true identity, you will be a better, kinder, and stronger person. You will become more effective and powerful than ever before. You will also be more successful in your community, in your organization and in your own business. K. L. Toth tells us, "One of the greatest tragedies in life is to lose your own sense of self and accept the version of you that is expected by everyone else." So, finding your true identity is your greatest weapon in this world. How are you going to achieve this?

Here are three questions that must be answered on this journey. The first question relates to your very nature. Do you really know your true identity? Who are you? Are you a collection of cells? Are you a body? What makes the difference between you and your family? For me, my identity is captured in three statements. I am a miracle. I am unique. I am a gift. I have a different personality. I always knew I was different from my brothers and sisters.

The second question relates to how you live your life. Are you living someone else's identity? You need to ask yourself: am I living someone else's dreams? Am I acting like someone else? Most of us are living the way our parents want us to live: go to college, get a job for 30 years and retire afterwards. But we each have our own identity, our dreams, and our own future. Since I was a child, I knew that I was an entrepreneur. You need to stop living someone else's dream. If you want to be a painter, go paint. If you want to join a club, go and join it. If you want to travel the world, do it. Go and find yourself. Who cares what others think about you? Follow your dreams.

The third question relates to your value. Why is your identity so important? Your identity is like a fingerprint. Your identity is the key to open up a whole new world for you and those around you. In answering this question, you will discover who you really are. This question is the key to opening your heart, your soul, and your mind. Your heart will lead you to reflect on the question: What do you love and have passion for? Your soul will ask the question: Who are you? Your mind will ask you: Do you have a picture of who you want to become? In life, you need to answer all the three questions.

Reflect

As you consider these three questions related to your identity, I would like you to take time for reflection. You might go to a quiet place within yourself and take a personal inventory of where you are right now.

✓ Where am I right now?

✓ Are you where you want to be? If not, why?

✓ How can you become conscious of your

hidden motives, hidden faults?

✓ Paint a portrait of the kind of person you want to become.

✓ What are your shortcomings?

✓ What are the things you want to strengthen about yourself?

✓ What goals and dreams do you have?

✓ What are the things you need to do differently?

The calling

I'm sure that during your time of reflection, you had something calling you to do more, be more, and to have more. That something is your true identity calling you, asking you questions that must be answered. Please take your time, there is no rush.

Do you know the nature of your true identity that is calling you? Your true identity is calling you to become the person you are meant to be. I cannot wait for you to start living the life you are meant to live. Once you start living your true identity, you will be sitting at the head of the table. Your true identity is the key to knowing your purpose and meaning in life. This is only the tip of the iceberg. Like Star Trek, you will go where no human being has gone before. Your true identity is not about motivation but transformation: transformation of your mind, soul and heart.

Once you find your true identity, you will become unstoppable. I remember when I started searching for my true identity, I was approximately 43 years of age. It was tough, since the old me was constantly fighting against the new me. I fought a fierce fight. It took years, but I did it. My true identity was calling and telling me there is much more in you than you know.

Finding yourself

Finding your true identity is like being reborn. People will see you differently. They will see a sparkle in your eyes. Your whole body language will change. When you enter a room, people will notice new things about you. While some people will love the way you've changed, others will miss the old times. This was my situation. People would tell me that they missed the old me. I would tell them that I don't miss the old Israel at all. The old me never accomplished anything. Since I found my true identity, I discovered I could become a public speaker, write books, and become a life coach. I have also set for myself bigger and higher goals. This is only the beginning. It might be hard finding your true identity but once you find it, it is worth it.

Your values

Your true identity also has to represent your values and beliefs. In her book *The Perfect You*, Dr. Caroline Leaf wrote, "[Identity is] crucial to a life well-lived; it is the theme of countless books, both classical and modern, fiction and non-fiction. It shapes some of the greatest masterpieces in the world of art and characterizes the world of education. It is a question that none of us can escape a question that can only be answered by the individual as an individual." True identity is very important in our lives. When you don't know your true identity, you are a slave. A slave to your own failed potential.

I believe with all my heart that this book is in your

hands for a reason. You have it to change your life. Your old ways haven't gotten you where you should be. You might be still in the same place. You might feel you are stuck. Albert Einstein once said, "We cannot solve our problems with the same thinking we used when we created them." Therefore, we need to change. We are like a caterpillar trying to turn into a butterfly. For this to happen, the caterpillar needs to undergo massive transformation. It is called metamorphosis. While in the cocoon, the caterpillar goes through 100% transformation from head to toe. The caterpillar changes everything: legs, body, arms, brain. After this transformation, it finds its true identity as a beautiful butterfly.

This transformation is worth the struggle. It is a long journey. When you come out of the metamorphosis, you will have a new identity. You will have beautiful wings to fly. This was my experience, and I am proud to share it with you.

Lost and found

Many people in this world are searching for their

identity. Most of them are searching for it outside themselves. If this is you, remember that you will not find your true identity in someone else but inside you. It can only be found inside you. Therefore, you need to invest time and resources to find it. This could be reading books, listening to audio materials, attending seminars, traveling, looking deep down inside yourself, or asking personal questions. It is important that you do this because it will open your mind to finding your true you. That is what happened to me when I joined Toastmasters. There I found my calling as a speaker, writer, and mentor. It changed my whole life.

Your true identity is priceless. Once you find your true identity, you will begin to recognize that there is more stored inside of you than you could ever imagine. There are things inside you that you need to discover. There are ideas, talents, wisdom, knowledge and problem-solving skills to mention a few. Just imagine yourself coming up with the next idea to change the world. Imagine giving people advice that will change their lives. You can be the greatest CEO or business owner of this generation just because you found your true identity. I had been labeled a loser, drug addict, and good for nothing.

All my life I lived a lie. I was living like someone else until I remembered the words of my dad, one of the few truly valuable things he did for me.

One day, when I was about seven years old, I was sitting on my dad's lap. I said to him, "Dad I'm important." My dad replied, "You are the most important person in this world." There was silence between us. Then my dad said, "Son, are you number one or number two?" I told my dad, "I'm number one." Then my dad said, "Don't you forget it." For years I never believed it because I was mislabeled until I found my true identity.

At last, I started believing that I was important and that I was number one. Finding my true identity meant that I was not rejected. It meant that I really was important and accepted. I want you to say out loud "I am important. I am number one." Don't you forget it. Finding your true identity will help you do what you are meant to do. It will help you create the life you deserve. It will convince you that you truly are number one. If you fail to find your true identity you will be wandering around like a headless chicken. I was like that chicken for years trying to figure out who I was and what my purpose was. Once I found my identity my eyes opened to a new world.

Don't let people mold you

Let me be blunt. There are people who want to mold you according to their image. They want to transform you to be like them. To have no purpose, no vision, no dreams and no future. These people have no clue who they are. They are operating from the outside instead of the inside. They do not want to discover their true identity because their life seems to have no meaning. As I said before, it is very important to listen and understand that the more you disregard your true identity the more you will live your life like someone else. These people live by dominating and shaping others, although they are empty shells themselves. Don't be like them.

Once you start to find your true identity, your confidence will grow stronger. I found this in *The Confidence Code,* by Kathy Kay and Claire Shipman. "Confidence is the purity of action produced by the mind free of doubt." What this means to me is that you can face doubt or fear. That you can really find who you truly are. I love that quotation because when I was finding my true identity, my confidence was growing. I was becoming stronger each day. The more you search the more you grow. The more you grow the stronger you become.

Searching for your true identity will have a life changing impact. You will never want to go back to your old way of thinking, talking and walking. The important thing to remember is that you will make mistakes. Your weaknesses will be exposed. You will fall and fail. It is how you see and respond to these adversities that really matters. For me, I had to learn the hard way. I stopped agreeing with the lies of other people and the lies I told myself. I had to rewire my brain. This is the challenge: to rewire and renew your mind. You will need to reprogram and reset.

Let me ask you a few questions. Do you think you can find your true identity? Why do you want to find your true identity? These are questions only you can answer. If you said yes, you made the right choice. If you said no, it is okay, but please keep reading books, keep asking questions, keep searching. Your true identity may surprise you. It may reveal itself. There are going to be moments when you connect with people who have already found their identity. You may feel uncomfortable while looking for yours. This is a wonderful learning opportunity. Give yourself the proper level of respect. Never feel intimidated in your quest to find your own identity. You have come too far to give up on your search. It is never too late to find your purpose and your identity.

As you reach for your true-self, write your thoughts down. This really helped me find myself. One day I was at home reflecting on my notes. I could not believe the lie I was living. All the notes were negative and nothing positive. I was writing things down like these: I'm nobody. I only have a GED. I'm not accepted. Then I wrote a question down: Do you still want to live a lie? I looked at the question for a while, then it hit me. I said, "No more living a lie!" I had to change quickly because I had no direction.

We need to stop living a lie. Look for a mentor. Find

someone who is more successful and experienced than you. You can do this. Remember, your mind will tell you that you cannot change. Resist that. You need to have a plan, a dream, and goals. A compass that will direct you. You need a blueprint of your destination even if you think it's stupid. Write it down. Then go back and reread it. You need to believe in yourself before you can change from head to toe. Remember that you are important. You are number one.

Manifest your identity

When people start seeing one's own true identity, they will begin to ask you questions. How did you change? Why? What caused the change in you? People will be drawn to you because you have discovered your voice. People need to hear your voice in the world. Finding your true identity will help you in unexpected ways. People who never listened to you will listen. People who never followed you will follow. People who never wanted to know you will ask about you. Finding your true identity will be powerful.

Some people are afraid of finding their true identity. Marianne Williamson says, "Our deepest fear is not that we are inadequate, our deepest fear is that we are powerful beyond measure." This is a very profound statement. It should give you goose bumps just knowing that you are powerful. Finding your true identity will make you powerful beyond measure by finding strength you didn't know you had. There is so much more in you so stop playing small. It is time to be big. Your true identity will pull you out of your comfort zone, your insecurities and your fears.

New Territory

You will step into unknown territory. It is there that you will find the missing pieces of your life. There, you will grow, feel pain, learn and change. There you are going to find your destiny and purpose. There your true identity will be awakened. Expect great things to happen in your life. The dreams you once had will be reborn.

Growing up I wanted to be Superman, Bruce Lee, Batman, even a teacher. We were not afraid to dress up as our favorite super hero because we didn't care what people said about us. Then we grew up and lost our imagination. We lost our identity. We are afraid of what people will say about us. We are afraid to dress up again. I tell you this, don't be afraid to dress up as a super hero again. You have bigger dreams and bigger goals. Who cares what people say!

In his book, *Expect Greatness*, John Hawkins writes, "We are meant for greatness." When I was pondering on this, I started believing with all my heart and soul that I have greatness within me. I can do greater things than I can ever imagine. But it won't happen overnight. It takes time and discipline.

You will learn new lessons and make more mistakes, but the good thing about it is that you will think differently. You will no longer solve the same problems with the old solutions. Like I said, there is a cost to finding our identity. A price we must pay.

Your identity is in your hands. It is your future. It is

time to build great things. If only I had this advice when I was younger I would have been substantially more successful. Remember, your past does not define you. Your new identity is your future. So find it. Finding it is essential if you want to succeed and go to the next level. Without it you will stumble through life. Your true identity is the key to your success. I urge you to give yourself permission to find your true identity. Before we proceed to the next chapter, here is my final question to you: What are three things that you would like to do once you find your true identity?

1_____

2_____

3_____

In the following chapters we will go deeper to transform your life.

Third Key: Prove People Wrong

"The best revenge is massive success."

~Frank Sinatra

After letting go of the past and finding your true identity, it is time to focus on the next key to transform your life. I have called this key 'Prove People Wrong'. This is based on one of my favorite quotations from Frank Sinatra, "The best revenge is massive success." It is my desire that this chapter will help you think in a different way. Proving people wrong is not about getting even but getting ahead in life. It is about moving forward. This chapter is for the people who made fun of you, criticized you, belittled you. It's for those who have told you that you are never going to make it. Here are the four things that will help you prove people wrong.

Fight the good fight

This is the first step to prove people wrong. There is no success without failure and rejection. You have to fight hard day and night for your success, your dreams, your vision. When someone becomes successful it is because they made a life-changing decision. Proving people wrong is a decision you need to make. What's your decision?

Once you start telling yourself and others what you want to accomplish, there is no turning back. People are going to remember your words. People are going to start throwing your past at you. You're going to hear about the person you used to be, the mistakes you have made, the promises you have broken, and the bridges you have burned. This is what happened to me. People brought out something I did 20 years ago. These were the people I needed to stay away from.

In proving people wrong, it is very important that you change who you are. A lot of people won't like it at all. Your character will change. You will separate from your old friends and from your old life style. You will act and think differently. Proving people wrong not only proves to others that you can make it but proves that you are doing your own detox from head to toe. When I did my own detox it was painful, but it was necessary. You will fight your inner demons. There is a saying "higher levels, bigger devils." You have to fight mentally. When life knocks you down, you get up. The punches of life are going to hurt you. What do you need to fight for? What is the battle in your mind that you need to win? What demons do you need to kill?

Integrity

Integrity is the quality of being honest and having moral principles or moral uprightness. It is a personal choice to hold oneself to consistent standards. When I read that I really knew I had a lot of work to do if I wanted to prove people wrong. I had to raise my standards. When I started having standards it opened a new life for me. My life has meaning now.

Allow me to share are a few ways my life changed since I started being a person of integrity. When I said something, I did it even if I hurt to do it. If I said yes I would keep my commitment. It is okay to say no to people. If you want to go after your dreams and goals, you must have integrity. That needs to be on top of your list if you want to prove people wrong.

Proving people wrong is a wonderful thing because it brings out the very best in you. You're now doing all the things that you thought you could never do. Integrity will lead you there. You need to start with baby steps. For example, be at work on time, pay all your bills on time, say what you are going to do, clean your car, and make your bed in the morning. Also, treat people with respect even if they do not respect you. Integrity gets you everything. Integrity is knowing what is right and doing it. All my life I lacked integrity. So, I started reading books on integrity, blogs, and anything I could find on it I read. And little by little I built my reputation as a person of integrity. It took me a long time, but I got there.

I also learned another very important thing. I was talking to myself, and the word stop came to me like a lightning bolt. So, I paused for a minute and said to myself, "Stop being lazy. Stop cheating yourself. Stop lying to yourself. Stop watching TV. Stop being average. Stop wasting your time. Stop hanging with the wrong people. Stop gossiping. Stop making excuses. Just stop." People with integrity don't waste time, they go after the things that must get done.

What is integrity for you? How can you improve your integrity? What are the changes you have to go through to improve your integrity? Building your integrity and keeping your promises is very important. Like a compass, integrity keeps you going in the right direction. Once you start breaking promises to yourself and to others your compass breaks, and then you have no direction. You are lost, and people will see this.

I was lost for a long time, I had a broken compass. I had to rebuild my compass and that was the hardest part. People did not believe me. So, I had to try harder to prove myself again and again. When people started seeing my integrity I was given permission to succeed in life.

Self-discipline

One difficult thing I had to do was discipline my mind and my body. This will be hard and uncomfortable in your journey. Even writing this book took a lot of discipline. I had to stop watching TV. I had to get up early to write. It also taught me a lot of things about myself. Most importantly, I learned that I have the power to do it. Do you have the power to start living a life of discipline?

If you have a vision or dream of going back to school, writing a book, or starting a business, it's going to take a lot of discipline. Discipline is the one thing that is going to separate you from others. Sometimes it's difficult to get up in the morning to go to the gym, eat right, read, study, get to school. It takes discipline to do all those things. I was lazy. I fought and made excuses. Excuses don't get you anywhere. Self-discipline is absolutely required if you want to be successful in any field you are in. It is the key that will help you grow. This key will help you to finish reading a book, complete a project, do your homework, or lose weight.

Do me a favor. This week, write the word discipline all over your house. All of those reminders will help you out. That is what I did, and I started seeing the change in me. If I wanted to eat sweets and drink diet sodas, I had the word discipline in the refrigerator. It is one little thing that will help you get the big things. What areas do you need discipline in? How can you improve your discipline? What projects or books have you not yet finished?

Commitment

Commitment means an agreement or pledge to do something in the future. That's a powerful definition. Once you commit to your dreams and your goals, you make an unbreakable pledge to yourself. Here are more powerful words that are related to commitment.

1. Faith
2. Devotion
3. Loyalty
4. Dedication
5. Attachment

You need to stay committed no matter what. If you fail, it's okay, but get up, because you have a commitment to your family, to your dreams and your goals. Be committed to yourself. That's what's important. Yes, unexpected things are going to happen. They happened to me. When I started writing this book, I got fired from my job but soon found another. My mother was sick, and I had to help her financially. The stress drained me so much, that my mind was tired. I worried how I was going to pay the bills, but I was still committed to writing this book. This is the sort of life lesson that we need to go through. Lessons in life will be thrown our way as if to see if we are committed. Do not take the easy way out. Stay committed, and go after that dream that you have in your heart.

When I was writing this book, I was working as a server in a restaurant. I was working my heart out to pay for this book, to build my brand, and to buy a website. It takes money to build a dream. It also takes hard work, long hours and long nights. I would stay up until four in the morning writing and thinking. You need to have your head up high and face the world. Even if I didn't have enough money, this book was going to get written one way or another. There is one word that commitment brings to my mind. That one word is strong. Even if no one is cheering you on, giving you a pat on the back, or saying good job. Stay strong and encourage yourself.

I could interview a lot of people on commitment and I would get a lot of different answers. I know you have your own answers. What does commitment mean to you? Write it in your own words.

1._____

2._____

3._____

Are you committed to your dreams? Are you committed to yourself? What do you need to be committed to?

Remember the 4 steps. Apply them to your life, and you will see the change in you. It's very important to prove people wrong. Just remember to fight the good fight, be a person of integrity, have self-discipline and stay committed no matter what.

Fourth Key: Speak Life not Death

The words that we speak create our world.

May I ask you a question? What words have you been telling yourself every day? What negative words are you saying about yourself? I believe in the power of words and what they can do in our lives and the lives of friends and families.

It does not matter what people say about you. What matters is what you say about yourself. You win or lose your battles by the words you say about yourself. Battles are won or lost in your words. I remember that I was in the gym one time and there was a lady next to me who was complaining that she could not lose weight. I asked her, "Why?" and she said, "I just can't." I said, "You need to start speaking life over yourself and not death." I told her that she could lose weight. "Instead of saying I can't, say I can." I also told her to get a piece of paper and pen. Every time she said something negative, she should write it down. Then at the end of the day, she should look at it to see how many times negativity had come out of her mouth. She told me she was going to start doing it.

If we could track the negative words that come out of our mouths, we all could write our own book. I wonder how many promotions, jobs, people that we want to meet and things that we want to do all pass us by just by saying to ourselves, "I'm not good enough. I am not talented. I am not that attractive."

Ugly words

Let me start by telling you a story about my dad and how his mother spoke death over him. My sister wrote an essay called *Dead Man Walking* about our dad. Hardly anyone stops to think about the fact that one day, our loved ones will leave this earth. It certainly never crossed my mind until I received the dreadful call in April 1997. My father was a man who once stood five feet eleven inches tall, slender and strong. He was a man of few words but held a great work ethic and was not too shy to say that he was number one. My father was also a very broken man, who drank too much to deal with guilt and immense pain. Sadly, he was a dead man walking for most of his life.

The guilt and the profound pain my father endured daily was from an incident that left his younger brother mentally disabled. This led to my father using alcohol to medicate the pain. Only in the state of inebriation could he find temporary relief. He was the eldest of five siblings and truly was number one until the day everything changed. My father was nine years old when my grandmother asked him to watch over his two-year old brother while she took care of some chores. Like any child his age, my father got distracted, and his brother, wanting to explore the world, ran to the neighbor's house. He was struck by their vehicle as they backed out of their driveway. My grandmother was hysterical and panic-stricken as she held her baby's lifeless body.

In her moment of agony, she shouted at my dad, "It's your fault," without considering the damage she would cause him. These words pierced his heart and scarred his soul. My father saw his little brother bleeding from the head, but the words of his mother cut deeper than the wounds of his little brother.

My father's ensuing alcoholism led to a fatal disease. I felt quite nervous when I went to meet with my dad, to discuss his worker's compensation claim and other personal business. I had no inkling how he had taken the news of his cancer diagnosis. I was indeed surprised to see him handling the news of the diagnosis quite well. At that point he was very fragile and thin, as if the disease had sucked every cell out of his body. He was a 53 year-old man who looked 70. He was holding on to hope as he was about to start chemo treatments.

It was afternoon when I went to visit my father. As I was driving up, I found him sitting outside enjoying the breeze of a summer day beneath the carport. My dad immediately reached out for my newborn baby. He placed her on his chest and rocked her back and forth. He seemed very peaceful, hopeful and ready to combat this awful disease. The reason for his confidence was that his younger brother had also been diagnosed with stomach cancer a year prior. After undergoing some chemo treatments, he was in remission. My father had the assurance that the same thing would happen to him, especially since he had a spirit-filled prayer warrior Pentecostal mother and all of the church family praying for him.

During the summer, I was quite busy with my newborn and with my other three kids. I still kept in touch with my dad. On numerous occasions, I asked my father how he was doing. He really never said much. I could never get him to open up and discuss his prognosis. Perhaps he didn't want me to know how sick he was, or he didn't want to face the reality that he was dying. As time passed, I could see him deteriorating rapidly, yet he still seemed hopeful. I heard him say to a family friend that the chemotherapy was the reason he felt so weak, though it was a necessary procedure.

Six months after his diagnosis of cirrhosis of the liver, I got a call early one morning from my grandmother. She said my dad had been moaning and not responding. I knew deep down it was the end, the finale for Mr. #1. As soon as I hung up with her, I called for the ambulance to take him from the house to the hospital. I rushed there and sobbed all the way while calling up family members. After I arrived at the hospital, I waited patiently for the doctor's prognosis. It felt like the longest wait I have ever been through, but it had only been an hour. It was enough time for the rest of the family to arrive. The doctor calmly walked into the lobby and said, "You know he's dying, so there's no need to poke him and run tests on him. Let him die in peace."

When the doctor said, "Let him die in peace," I instantly remembered a dream I'd had months prior to first finding out about my dad's illness. This dream had been embedded in my heart, but was dormant, until the magic word peace was spoken.

In this dream, I recalled an audible voice that spoke to me. Instantly, I knew it was the Lord. He said that my dad had to do three things so he could die in peace. He had to ask for forgiveness, forgive and let go of the past. At first, I didn't think much about the dream because I dream all the time. Beyond that, my dad had not yet been diagnosed with cancer. He was definitely depressed but not ill. In fact, I witnessed all three things. A week prior to his death, I was at the hospital with my sister, visiting him after he'd had his last chemo treatment. As we were talking a minister walked in, very excited, and said, "Sister, your father asked God for forgiveness and surrendered his life to the Lord." Right after the minister left I asked my dad, "Have you forgiven yourself?" He said yes. He shared that he had also asked my mother for forgiveness. I told him the act of forgiveness would allow the bondage of pain and guilt to break away and not hold him hostage anymore. He nodded his head in agreement.

I honestly believe that my father would have been a better spouse and father if it had not been for his mother's harsh words. This story about my dad is a great example of the power of words: how his mother spoke death over him. The wound was so deep in his soul that the roots of grief, bitterness, anger, sadness, betrayal and unforgiveness took over his life. It is possible that we, his children, got the bitter fruit of it. Just imagine speaking death over your child or anyone else. The repercussions can last a lifetime.

I have heard family and friends and even teachers speak death over me. You are just like your father. You are drinking yourself to death. You are never going to accomplish anything in life. You are a failure. You are a loser. Many people have spoken such words over my life before. For years, I carried those words with me. I, too, had developed roots of anger and bitterness. My family also saw the repercussions of this: skipping school, doing drugs, joining gangs, becoming a crack addict, and beating my wife. Negative words clung to me like a disease. People remember words or phrases spoken to them long ago. Those words still haunt them even today. I know people who remember what their parents told them twenty or thirty years ago.

I gave a speech one day and told people about the power of negative words. I said, "just image holding sand in your hands and then throwing it in the air." I then asked them to imagine picking up the sand one grain at a time. You cannot do it. Once you release negative words, you cannot get them back. Be careful what you say to yourself and others.

Breaking the curse

It took me years to overcome the words spoken over my life. I needed to turn those words into life, but I didn't know how. So, I started reading books on the power of words, listening to CDs and anything I could find about the power of words. One day I went to a small church in Texas. The pastor was preaching on the power of words. He got my attention. That day changed my life. He started out with Proverbs 18:21, "Death and life are in the power of the tongue, and they that love it shall eat the fruit of it." I said wow! I was eating the bitter fruit that people had spoken over my life. I was also eating the fruit that I was speaking over myself, all those years of speaking death. Instead of planting my own seeds of death and destruction, I started planting new seeds for my future. I needed to change my words. I had a lot of weeds that needed to get pulled out.

Creating your own world

It was hard to change my words and myself. I had created my own dark and miserable world by my own words. I needed to change my world, my life and my future by changing the words I said about myself. I knew it was going to be a long road ahead of me, but it had to be traveled. I needed to plant great things in my life with my words. Remember, people had spoken many negative things in my life and I believed them. I was feeling worthless and like a loser in life. Those negative words that people spoke to me kept popping up again and again. I would say I am blessed, then my mind would say how can you be blessed if you have nothing? Then I would say I walk in favor, then my mind would say again, no one likes you. But I kept on and on until I started to believe in myself again. Once I started changing my words, my life started changing as well, slowly but surely. Change your words and change your life!

I started doing self-talk. I started repeating words over my life and over my future. We are what we think and say. So, I started filling my mind with positive words. In a very real sense, we reap what we sow in our minds. Positive thoughts produce positive words and results. Negative thoughts produce negative words, actions and results. How we direct our thinking, self-talk, and attitude determines which way we go. It is therefore important that we carefully choose our words, for they bring life or death.

I would like for you to do me a favor. I want you to go to a public place and listen to people talk. Listen to how many negative words come out of their mouths. I went to a coffee shop one day and right next to me were three ladies talking about their husbands. I heard words such as "He is too fat... Lazy... Not good in bed... Never does anything around the house..." Some ladies went on and on talking really bad about their husbands, but one lady refused to talk bad about her husband. She said that he is kind, loving, listens to her even if he comes home late at night. He still makes time for her. And not one negative word came out of her mouth. As I was just listening, I said wow, she is wonderful. However, the other three ladies were belittling their marriage, their husbands, and were busy planting many seeds of destruction in their minds and hearts. If you are doing that to your wife, husband, children or family, it is time to stop.

In his book, *In Him, S.P.E.A.K,* Kenneth Hagin writes, "You always get and have in your life what you believe and say. If you do not believe what you are saying, you should not say it, because if you say something long enough, those words eventually will register on your spirit and control your life." Words are powerful. We are shaped by our words. Words shape our future. This is the formula that I came up with and it worked for me. I will share it with you. I was sitting on my recliner with a pen and my notebook, asking the Lord for help. The word SPEAK was dropped in my heart and I wrote it down.

The acronym SPEAK means:

- ✓ Specific
- ✓ Purpose
- ✓ Existence
- ✓ Align
- ✓ Keep Going

Specific

In the dictionary, specific means unique, specialized, orders given, to be clear, to be understood, and straightforward. So, we need to be specific as to what we say about ourselves and our future. This is an exercise for you to be specific. To help you do this, you might want to complete the following exercise.

I can_____

I can_____

I can_____

I am_____

I am_____

I am_____

I will_____

I will_____

I will_____

I started doing this and it changed my life. I got three index cards and I wrote: **I can____, I am____,** and **I will____,** Then I filled in the words:

✓ I can lose weight.

✓ I can start my own company.

✓ I can write a book.

✓ I can start my business.

✓ I can make a difference.

I would say, I can come up with new ideas, I can solve problems. The next day I would say throughout the day:

✓ I am great.

✓ I am strong.

✓ I am smart.

✓ I am wise.

✓ I am bold.

Then I got my other index card and said:

✓ I will make it.

✓ I will be debt free.

✓ I will raise my family to live with integrity

✓ I will make it at all costs.

✓ I will study, read and learn

✓ I will be the first author in my family.

I hope this activity has given you the time to reflect on the power of words. This changed my whole life just saying specific words over myself. I started acting and seeing things differently. Everything started changing once I began changing my words. I began speaking life. I was careful what words came out of my mouth. My faith started to increase. I saw what I spoke about come alive in front of me. I started saying I'm an author, speaker, and entrepreneur. All three came true. This book is the fruit of my words.

Start speaking life over yourself, family, and business. I promise that you will see the difference. Start speaking things that you want to happen in your life. Words are life and death. Build yourself up with powerful words, and they will change your life. Remember words are like arrows. Point them where they need to go.

The opposite of specific is uncertain, lost, careless, unspecific, difficult to catch, and confuse. When people can't speak words that give life they will come up with excuses. I was talking to my sister the other day. We were talking about her goals. I asked her, do you have your goals written down? What are you going to do with your degree? She said, "I don't know." I then told her, "Did you know that 'I don't know' has a cousin named 'someday,' and a sister called 'I'll start tomorrow,' that has an uncle named 'I'll start on Monday,' that has an aunt called 'I'll start on the first of the month'?" I advised my sister to stay away from that kind of family. I told her to write down what she wants to do with her degree.

I remember when I was a child, I used to go to an abandoned building and say my name. I loved hearing the echo of my name, Israel. I used to say, "You are superman!" And the echo would say back "You are superman!" One day my brother said I was not superman and guess what I did. I went back to that abandoned building and I said to myself, "You *are* superman!" and the echo came back repeating my exact words. I was specific with the words I was saying to myself.

Do you really want all the negative things you've been saying to yourself and your family to come to pass? Negative words can have a lasting impact far beyond one person, like the words spoken over my father. Those negative words impacted him from his childhood on. Do you remember the saying, "Sticks and stones will break my bones, but words will never hurt me"? That is a big fat lie. Do you remember just once when one negative word was spoken to you as a child? I can. I remember my third grade teacher telling me that I was dumb. Then my high school teacher said that I would never accomplish anything. Those words hurt me for a long time.

Purpose

The word purpose means aim, design, goal, dream, plan, or target. Your words need to have purpose. There are three things you need in order to have words that are purpose-filled. First, you need a strong mind. You need to fill your mind with pictures of what you want to accomplish. I called it a vision board. I have pictures of people whom I want to meet and books I want to read.

Second, you need a strong heart. You need to have the heart to follow your purpose. You have to love yourself first. Lots of people never reach their goals because they do not have a strong heart. There are millions of people complaining about their lives, not knowing that they have the power to change. Once people start loving themselves, they can change their entire lives. It is time for you to move towards your purpose. Your purpose is to grow. Do not stay in a place where you are not growing. You need to dig up your roots and plant yourself were you can grow.

The third thing you need is a strong vision. You need to make that vision real in your heart and in your soul. Dress up and walk like your vision is manifesting before your eyes. When people ask you what is up with you, tell them that you are walking with vision.

We have control over the words that come out of our mouths: words of doubt or words of faith. Your words have purpose. Your words need a target. Your words have meaning since everyone has a purpose in this world. And your purpose starts with your words. You can redesign your life with your words.

Purpose is not a duty. It is an obligation. One purpose in my life is to be debt free and have a nice home. I never had a nice home growing up. As a young boy, I was a migrant worker for many summers. I grew up poor. I used to sell tomatoes and lettuce to my neighbors. I even used to pick up used cans and sell them at a recycling center. At the same time, I had so much fun. I knew I had more inside me. Here are some questions for you:

✓ Do you see yourself being debt free?

✓ Do you see yourself changing your life?

✓ Do you see yourself owning a business?

✓ Do you see yourself going back to school?

If you have said yes to any of these questions, you have a purpose. I believe that each one of us has a purpose in this life. A purpose that God has given you and you only. Your purpose is maybe to become a better father, a better husband, or open your own business.

Existence

Existence relates to life, want, currency, presence, real world, ideas, and wisdom. The opposite of existence is death. Your words create life or destroy life. When we start speaking the things we want in our life, we start creating them with our words. We create pictures in our minds. Words create pictures. You bring your dreams and your vision into existence. This is powerful. So, be careful what you say and never destroy your dreams by saying you can't. Those words "you can't" are the most powerful words out there. There are many people who kill their dreams simply by saying, I can't.

I believe half of the battles in life are in words. I read a book long ago about a cancer survivor who would say aloud, "I will live and not die." Over and over again, daily, she would speak words of life and health over herself. Over time, she became completely healed of cancer while other patients were dying. It is a choice to bring life to existence or to die. I would encourage you to start having pictures of your dreams and your vision on the wall and say to yourself, "This will come to pass. I will make it happen in my life." I have a vision wall and I have a check-list of places I want to visit and people I want to meet. And I say, "I will go to those places and meet those people."

Align

Align means to join, and to come across. The opposite of align is mess up, disjoin, disorder, and divide. If you say that you are going to accomplish a dream and a goal, start aligning your words with it. That is what I did. You need to align yourself with your mind. Align yourself with people who have the same mentality as you. Align yourself with powerful words. Stop saying that you are not smart enough. Start saying you *are* smart enough. Just imagine what you can do if you can walk your talk. You can change your world.

I have a vision wall in my office with pictures of my business name. I have a world map with thumbtacks on those places I want to visit. I have magazines where I want to be published. I created a powerful vision that I have to align myself with and that is hard to do because I had to change my whole life. It is a fight between the old you and the new you. Aligning your life with this new vision will take a new mindset plus a lot of discipline. It is going to be hard, but it is possible.

Aligning yourself in a different direction will change your life. It is like finding a treasure. Remember to align yourself with people who also can speak in your life. In what ways can you change your words? How can you align yourself with new people? How can you align yourself with your dreams and your goals?

Keep

This is the last letter in the acronym S.P.E.A.K. Keep relates to maintain, feeding, custody, and care. These words are important in your life if you want to fulfill anything you want in life. The opposite is neglect, ruin, harm, and destruction. These words are dangerous. If you keep saying negative and ugly words about your life and your dreams, you will destroy your whole life. We therefore need to protect our lives. No matter what you are going through you can change your life around by your words. Stop harming and destroying your future with your words. No matter what happens, keep speaking Specific words in your life. Keep speaking Purpose in your life. Keep speaking words of Existence. Keep Aligning your words with your dreams. And when the going gets hard in life, Keep on speaking life.

It's great to speak life, but you will need to speak life to your dream more than once to give your dream life. Your consistency to speak life to your dream will depend on where you are with giving life to your dream. If your dream is brand new, you will need to speak several times a day to remind yourself of what needs to be done to make it a reality. If your dream is close to being a reality, you may not have to speak as often. But remember, no one will speak life into your dream but you.

1. What dreams do you need to speak life to?
2. Are you speaking life to your family, your spouse and children?
3. Are you speaking life to yourself?
4. How consistently should you speak life to your dreams?

Fifth Key: Develop Good Habits

"We first make our habits, and then our habits make us." ~John Dryden

This quotation is so true and powerful. Habits can make us or break us. I learned that habits can determine our lives. Habits can teach us a lot about ourselves. If we are not disciplined and not focused, habits can tell a lot about where we are in life. In this chapter, we are going discuss some habits that will help you grow.

Reading Books

This is the first habit. Get in the habit of reading books. This is important to your growth and your success. I read about three books a month, and this has greatly helped me grow. Reading books has helped me think and act differently. One thing for sure, it will help you find some answers. I started considering the authors of the books I read my "far-away mentors."

I always tell the people I mentor to read all the books in your field. If you are a CEO, read all you can on leadership and communication. If you are a teacher, read all you can about childhood development. If you are a manager, read all the books you can on people skills. Books will change the way you live. Your conversation, your leadership style and your innermost thinking will not be the same.

This habit of reading books will change your life the way it did for me. I built a library. Think about what books you need to read. Make a list and start acquiring them one by one. For instance, I worked in the restaurant business for over 30 years. I have read many books on customer service and people skills that helped me serve the guests better. I would advise you to create a habit of reading books. Learn from the wisdom of others that is out there waiting for you. It is essential for your growth.

Fail big and quickly

This is the second habit. This is what most people are afraid of. They are afraid of taking risks. Failure must happen in your life if you want to grow. Take all your mistakes in stride. I always tell people that paper and pen do not forget. Write all your mistakes and failures down, so you can go back and review them and ponder on them. That way you know what you can do differently next time. Do not be afraid to swim in the pool of failure. It will get you out of your comfort zone and strengthen your thinking. It is failure that will make you stronger, wiser and more knowledgeable. Your past failure will be replaced by something better.

I always say it is not failure, it is a lesson learned. This helped me every time I failed. I would ask myself, what lesson did I learn? What skill do I need to sharpen? What classes do I need to take? Everyone on top was once on the bottom. They learned a lot of lessons from their mistakes. What are you afraid of? Make a list of the things you are afraid of failing at. My advice is find people who have been there and ask them questions such as, how did you overcome this fear? What steps did you take?

I was afraid to write this book, but I asked other authors about the first time they wrote. Their best advice was to keep writing. It's okay to fail. Then I asked, what happens if my book doesn't sell? My friend's response was, what do you think happens if it does sell?

Respect

This is the third habit. We all crave respect. No matter who we are, we find it difficult to respect others when they don't respect us. Self-respect is about amassing a deep sense of worth and self-love. It's about knowing that you are worthy to receive and give respect. Respect can never be bought or demanded. It has to be earned. One of the necessary conditions to gain respect is to give respect. This is a very important habit to develop in your career. Respect yourself and others will respect you back. This habit is critical. A person who does not respect himself or herself can never hope to win the respect of others. In other words, if you don't value yourself, nobody will value you.

Once you start to respect yourself people will notice it. Respecting yourself will bring confidence, pride in yourself, and your self-esteem will develop. It will show in the way you walk, talk, and the way you carry yourself. People can see your self-respect as you walk by them on the street. But don't confuse it with egotism. People can see that right away too. It is equally important that you respect the opinions of others.

My question to you is: Do you respect yourself? Yes or no. If not, why? How can you change that? I never respected myself because I had a low self-image for years. I had to learn to respect and love myself. It took years to learn how, but here is how I did it.

1. I learned to love myself.

2. I stopped toxic relationships.

3. I stopped feeling sorry for myself.

4. I took responsibility for my life and world.

There is much more about respect that I could go into. This is something that you need to find for yourself. Respect goes a long way. It is give and take. No matter what, there are people that are not going to respect you back. But that does not mean you do not respect them.

Asking questions

"If you don't ask, the answer is already no," says Sarah Kathleen Peck. This is the fourth habit to develop. Asking questions might sound stupid to others. They might give you a dumb look or even roll their eyes. Asking questions is important if you want to learn, grow, and understand. I love asking questions if I do not know the answer. Trust me, if I'm unsure, I'm asking. I ask until I find the answer.

New research suggests that you can tell a lot about a person by the questions he or she asks. In particular, there is a difference between people who ask questions and people who do not. People who ask questions get more informed and their intelligence improves. They get better ideas for solving problems. They are more likeable in the workplace. People who do not ask questions never get answers. There is nothing wrong in asking questions because you want to find the answers.

When I was area director for Toastmasters, I had five clubs that I needed to cover. I had no idea what to do. So, I started asking questions—I mean a lot of questions—until I found the answers. There is no such thing as a dumb question. I read a book once that said the smartest people in the world started off by asking questions. Warren Buffet once said that when he started out his career, if he didn't know the answer, he would ask until he found it. Therefore you do not need to be afraid of asking questions.

Ask more questions than ever. Don't be afraid. You'll find the answers. Asking questions will help you connect with other people. When I started my business and writing, I asked other entrepreneurs and authors how they started. The advice they gave me saved me a lot of time. Plus, I was introduced to other authors just by asking questions. When asking a question, be clear and be direct. Think about the question, think about it again, and write it down. Maybe you need to rephrase the question.

I remember one time I asked a question about my book. I said, "What do you think about this?" My mentor said, "Think about what? You're not giving me a question. Be more direct. Be specific. Ask, for example, 'What do you think about my title and subtitle?' That is a question."

If you don't ask, you don't receive. It's that simple. Still, a lot of people are afraid to ask questions. Maybe they're afraid they might not like the response. Maybe it's a stupid question. Who cares? Ask the question anyway. Asking questions helps you get ahead of other people.

Write things down

This is the fifth habit you need to develop. Neuroscience explains why you need to write down your goals, vision, and thoughts. This helps you remember. I always tell people that paper and pen do not forget. I am sure you have heard that to achieve anything in life you need to write it down.

If only I could go back and write down all the ideas I've had. This thought has occurred to me many times. I always say I will remember, then later forget. When you write down your ideas you automatically focus your full attention on them. Few if any of us can write one thought and think another at the same time. Thus, a pencil and paper make excellent concentration tools.

Here are some reasons and tips to help you write things down:

- Always have a notebook with you that can fit in your pocket or purse. Having a notebook with you is important because you can write down a sudden idea, write down a quotation, or the title of a book, no matter where you are.

- Sleep with your notebook. You can have an idea in the middle of the night. This has happened to me a lot. I have written down some ideas and titles for my future books just because I had a notebook next to the bed.

- Always go back and review your notes, ideas, etc. When I go back and review my notes, I always come up with new idea.

- Writing helps you to connect with your thoughts. So, just write. Writing helps me connect with my words, and I can give closer attention to my ideas.

- Writing connects your brain to the words that you wrote. This helps me paint a picture in my brain of how my next project will look.

- Writing things down will help you start your journal. I have four journals that I started years ago. Writing in them has helped me grow and keep track of my thoughts.

- Writing things down tells you that you care about yourself and your future. It gives you space to think big and aim high. No matter what's going on in our outside world, when we write things down, we enter a world of possibility. It shows that you care about your future.

- Writing things down will help you plan ahead and give you a head start. Writing things down gives me a starting point. It can be the foundation for building something new and big.

This list is a jumping off point for you. What other things would you add to this list? Do you have a habit of writing things down? If not why?

Believing

This is the sixth habit: Start believing in yourself. This habit will help you greatly in your journey. When you start believing in yourself you will leave the discomfort zone behind. Learn to trust yourself and go make your mark. When I started writing, a lot of people would say, "You, Israel? You're writing a book?" I would say, "Yes!" So, I would start every day by saying, "I believe in myself." I would repeat that to myself a hundred times a day. I do not care what people say about me anymore. Why? Because I believe in myself. And that's indispensable. If you want to live a life of meaning and achieve your dream, you must believe in yourself and your ability.

Here are two daily habits that have consistently helped me increase my belief in myself. First, talk to yourself like an overcomer. I say, "I'm the greatest speaker on the planet. People will buy my books." Second, I carry an index card in my wallet with the word Believe. Every time things don't go my way or things go wrong, I pull out my card and look at that word. I meditate on it again and again until my faith revives. What about you? Do you believe in your dream? Why? If you don't believe, why?

Associate with successful people

Matt Enright says, "If you want to be successful, surround yourself with successful people." This seventh habit is vital. One of the most important decisions we make in life is who we choose to be around. In fact, there is an old proverb that reads, "Show me your friends and I'll tell you who you are." We often become like the people we're around. Based on that, we must be careful about whom we surround ourselves with because of the short-term and long-term implications. The people we associate with help determine how far we go in life.

Maybe that's a bit extreme. Are you hanging out with successful people? People who are more successful than you? Or are you hanging around with people who are equally as successful as you? Or are you spending your time with people less successful than you? These questions must be answered.

If you want a successful marriage, you don't go to someone who has been divorced two or three times. If you want advice for your business, you don't go to someone that doesn't have one. You go find and make a strong relationship with a successful businessman or woman. You buy them dinner and ask for their advice.

If you hang around with losers, guess what happens! Hang around with average people and you'll be average, too. But when you hang around with successful people, they will help you grow and think differently. That's what I did. I associated with people who were smarter than me. Because I wanted to be successful in my business, I listened to them speak and watched how they walk and how they communicate. I asked what books, blogs and articles they read. I wanted to know what they know.

This habit is vital to your success. It's a piece of the puzzle you cannot do without.

In this chapter, we learned the importance of creating new habits. The habits of reading books, failing big, respecting, asking questions, writing things down, believing, and associating with successful people. What other habits do you think you should develop for yourself? I hope they can help you to live your best life.

Sixth Key: Live Your Best Life

"You are the most important person in the world." -Dad

You need to live your best life. I am bursting with enthusiasm, energy and a desire to share what has happened to me. These three steps changed my life forever and for the better. This key opens life lessons that helped me live a better life and see the world in a different way. There are moments in life when you know you need to change. Your heart and your soul will tell you it's time. They remind you day and night that it is time to change your life because being the same does not get you anywhere. I had to make tough choices. Here are some lessons I learned along the way.

Stop complaining

The first step in living your best life is to stop complaining. People hate complainers. I was one of them. I was always blaming others. I was thinking I was better than them. I would complain about being broke, overweight, my job and many other things. Then someone told me, "You are complaining because you are not complete." I said, "What do you mean, I'm not complete?" The answer came, "It is because you're not living the life you want, and you do not want to work for it." That day changed my life.

Complaining was my way of inviting people to feel sorry for me and agree with what I was saying. From that day on, I started being more grateful. If I wanted a better life, I knew I had to change my thinking, my attitude, and my words. Complaining was poisoning my life. Complaining does not solve problems. Complaining pushes people away. Complaining affects your thinking. Complaining affects your self-esteem. So stop complaining. It will get you nowhere.

I did a challenge to stop complaining for 30 days. It was hard. It changed me. Just listening to complainers was a revelation. I was surprised to recognize myself. People will complain about the simplest things. Les Brown said something so powerful, "Surround Yourself with OQP i.e. Only Quality People." This changed me too. I started staying away from complainers and started only hanging around with quality people. If you want to live your best life now, stop complaining and start living. You also need to be grateful for the things you have. I wrote a list of the things I was grateful for: my life, my family, my job, my house and many others. This must replace the things you complain about.

Change yourself

The second step to live your best life is to change. Nothing changes until you change. I always hear people say, I wish I was more like him or her. I wish was taller, skinnier, and smarter. Remember, you are unique, you are one of a kind. There is no other "you" and that's what makes you special. Being yourself means that you must ask, what do I really need to change about myself? What can I change to be better?

As for me, that is what I did. I looked deep in my soul and said, "What do I need to change to become better?" I did a lot of soul searching. And it was not easy. I had to change my thinking if I wanted to live a better life. I needed to change my friends as they were not helping me grow. I needed new friends that would push me to reach my goals. I needed to change how I saw myself. I needed to picture in my mind a better future for myself and my family. Ask yourself the questions I asked: Do you need to change the way you think and why? Do you need to change your friends and why? Do you need to paint a better future for you and your family?

I used to be that person for a long time not loving myself until I made a decision that I would love myself. I started laughing more. I started going on dates with myself. I would get dressed up and feel loved. Have you noticed that when you get dressed up you feel different? I have seen all those TV shows when guys and girls have a hundred percent make over and you see that smile on their faces. Change is important and necessary if you want to live a better life.

Distance yourself from those who bring you down. If your relationships are not improving you, change them. Know your worth! When you give yourself to those who disrespect you, you lose. Your friends in life should motivate, inspire and respect you. Your circle should be well rounded and respectful.

Remember this step is important because, once again, if you don't change nothing changes.

Attitude

The third lesson is your attitude. This is a secret ingredient if you want to live your best life. A great attitude is absolutely essential for living a great life. Knowing this will help you to fulfill your dreams, goals and whatever you want to accomplish in life. Attitude will make you or break you.

Your attitude is a form of expression of yourself. Your attitude tells a lot about you. Attitude is your best friend or your worst enemy. Most of my life I had a really bad attitude. My attitude closed many doors for me. I was a waiter for many years and my attitude got in the way. I was not respecting my co-workers and I got fired for being rude.

Your good attitude will take you to great places and open doors for you. One thing I learned is that a negative attitude creates an atmosphere of distrust with family and co-workers. Family members can trust you when you always have something constructive to say. I've been around a lot of people that have bad attitudes. This is what I do: I keep quiet because you can't change them at all. I have seen this for so many years. A bad attitude destroys.

If you want outstanding results, have a great attitude and associate with people who have great attitudes. I did find a lot of great people with great attitude when I joined Toastmasters. My attitude changed for the better and I decided to change. When life throws you a brick, build a house. That is what people with great attitudes do. People with negative attitudes throw the brick back, and this hurts other people.

What kind of attitude do you have? Positive or negative? Has there been a time in your life when your attitude has opened doors or closed them for you? What kind of attitude are you exposed to at work? Remember, your attitude will make you or break you. Winston Churchill said it best, "Attitude is a little thing that makes a big difference."

I hope these three lessons you have just read will help you to start living your best life. First, quit complaining. People hate complainers. Second, change. For nothing changes until you change. Third and last, have a positive attitude. For your attitude makes or breaks you.

Seventh Key: Keep Moving Forward

"You, me or nobody is gonna hit as hard as life. But it ain't about how hard you hit. It's about how hard you can get hit and keep moving forward."

~Rocky, Sylvester Stallone

We have come to the end of this book, and I hope you have enjoyed reading it.

In the first key to transform your life, you focused on letting go of the bitterness, unforgiveness, failures, past, grudges and the pains. If we keep holding on to the past, there is no future. You will always be in the same place. It's important to let it go and *keep moving forward.*

In the second key, you found your true identity. This allowed you to find your new purpose, your belonging, your true you, and start living your dreams. Your new identity opens new doors for you. Remember, you have to lose your old self to find your new self. Finding your true identity becomes a journey for self-discovery and reveals your true purpose, your values and your standards. Discovering your true identity is a long and painful journey, but you have to put all your heart into it. You will hit road blocks, failure, slander and setbacks, but keep moving forward.

The third key to transform your life was PPW: Proving People Wrong. You needed to do this so that you could succeed and make your dreams come true. It will not be easy, but it is possible with hard work. People will hate you because you have changed and are not like them anymore. PPW says, "I'm going to make it." PPW is about hard work, putting in long hours and creating a new you. It is about leaving a legacy behind and a mark in this world. When people ask you how you succeeded, you can tell them your story. There will be people who will not like you because you have set higher standards for yourself. Remember to keep moving forward.

The fourth key focused on speaking life, not death. Words are very important in our life and to those around us. Speaking life to ourselves about our future brings great benefits such as confidence and great self-esteem. I always tell people that words are like plant food and we are the plant. If we speak life, we will grow and flourish. If you speak death you die. You are not feeding and watering your life with living words. As I said, words are like arrows. You point them where you want them to go. Keep speaking life over yourself, your dreams, your visions, and to your family. No matter what happens, keep moving forward.

The fifth key focused on creating new habits. We discovered that creating new habits is a life-changer. Changing little things at a time will make a big difference in your life. Start setting some small goals like getting up early or finish reading a book. Creating new habits is going to set you apart. Once you start creating new habits your bad habits will fade away. Be patient in creating new habits. It will take time to create them, but it is worth it in the end. You might get mad at yourself because some habits are hard to develop but keep moving forward.

The sixth key provided an opportune moment for you to reflect on the ways to live your best life. It talked about the three lessons that changed my life. First, quit complaining. In the end, you have control. Second, change is necessary, for nothing changes until you change. This is hard because change means everything from friends to family and yourself. Making changes will mean making hard decisions about yourself. It helped me to make a list of the things I needed to change. They were not easy, but I did change them. Some people did not like it because I was not one of them anymore. Third and last is attitude. Remember that attitude is everything. With the right attitude you can begin to achieve your dreams and your visions, and keep moving forward.

Now the seventh and final key to transform your life is the advice I always got from my mother. Even as a gang member, dropout, divorcé and someone who was in a half-way house and hit rock bottom, my mom would always tell me *Keep Moving Forward ("adelante, mijo")* These words helped me go through thick and thin. These words saved my life.

One important lesson I learned is, never give up. I remember one time I was walking alone and praying. I was going over a rough road both literally and spiritually. As I was walking, God spoke to my heart and said, "You are walking." "You are walking forward. You are not walking backwards or standing still. You are walking forward."

Those words gave me strength in my heart and in my soul. No matter what happens to you, keep moving and keep walking forward.

There are going to be people who want to kill your dreams and your vision. Tell them, I am moving forward. There is a price to pay when you keep moving forward. Confucius said, "The man who says he can, and the man who says he cannot are both correct." There are going to be days when you want to quit, hide, or give up. Remember to keep moving forward. This is not for the faint of heart but for the believer. Do you believe that you can *keep moving forward?* It is a journey that will make you mad, sad, and weep, but in the end you will smile.

I have a sister who keeps moving forward. She is a mother and a wife. She has four children, two of whom live at home. Also, she runs a business and studies for her degree at the same time. One thing about my sister is that she never complains at all. She keeps moving forward no matter what, even if she stays awake until one in the morning doing homework. Moving forward is for people who want a better life.

There is no shortcut if you want to succeed. There is

no other way around it. Moving forward is for people who are going to put in seconds, minutes, hours, days, weeks, months and years. There are people that do not want to keep moving forward. That is okay but you are not one of them. The people who keep moving are the ones who know what they want to become and the changes that they have to make.

The people who keep moving forward are world changers. When there is no path they make one and people follow. I am making my own path in this world and this book is that example. I never thought in a thousand years that I would write a book. But one day I'm going to travel the world and speak to thousands of people from all over. I believe.

I made my own path and I have kept moving forward no matter what. Even when I didn't have any money, I kept writing, reading and studying. I knew in my heart that I had to write this book. Those words from my mom helped me out: **KEEP MOVING FORWARD**. I would like to end with one of my favorite quotations from Martin Luther King Jr that gives me momentum to move forward.

Martin Luther said, "If you can't fly then run, if you can't run then walk, if you can't walk then crawl, but whatever you do you have to keep moving forward."

Conclusion

I have enjoyed writing this book, part autobiography but mostly advice from lived experience. If you heed my advice and follow even half of my recommendations, you will be a better person. Please give it a try, because, above all, I want you to KEEP MOVING FORWARD!

Keep Moving Forward

Keep Moving Forward

ABOUT THE AUTHOR

Israel Hernandez has persevered through life, defying odds in the face of adversity. Born in south Texas, USA as the fifth of eight children to migrant working parents, Israel's difficulties in life and in identity began right away. His hostile relationship with his alcoholic father, combined with verbal abuse and negativity from educators and administrators would help pave the way for a life of bad decisions, violence, and substance abuse.

Israel's massive life changes began shortly after moving to San Antonio to get away from drugs and violence, as well as the people that were enabling the problems. He continued a life in the service industry and studying communication and leadership. In over thirty years in the business, Israel has not only helped restaurants properly train new people, but also made unmatched connections with patrons. He has also leveraged his studies to become a competitive speaker with Toastmasters.

Transformation is possible with the right mindset and choices made. Israel is living proof and shares his keys to keep moving forward in this book.

For information on Israel speaking at your business, church,
or convention please visit:
www.IsraelSpeaks.com
Email: Tee@israelspeaks.com
Call: 210-686-5508